MOTLEY the CAT
From "Wright Angles"

"Round Up the Usual
Cat Suspects"

By LARRY WRIGHT

**INTRODUCTION
By MIKE PETERS**

Stabur Press, Inc.

Published by Stabur Press, Inc., 23301 Meadow Park, Redford, MI 48239

ISBN: 0-941613-09-7

3 5 7 10 8 6 4 2

Printed in the United States of America

INTRODUCTION

I hate Larry Wright!

I mean he's a successful comic strip cartoonist, he does great editorial cartoons, he's even an associate editor of the Detroit News Editorial Page.

Cat lovers love Larrry Wright! Cat lovers are, after all, a special breed. They are insanely devoted to their cats. And sometimes they hate their cats. Either way they all love Motley because he's a real cat — he thinks cat thoughts and eats real birds. In fact, Motley embodies all the facets of cat life — or should I say, all the Angles.

Maybe I should join Wright Angles Anonymous.

Mike Peters

For Dad

WRIGHT ANGLES

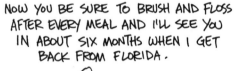

© 1986 United Feature Syndicate, Inc.

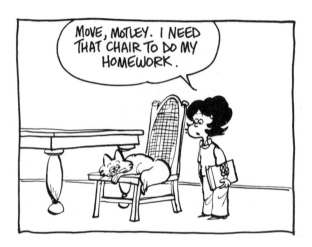

CHOMP!

POP

I WISH I HAD A SNAPSHOT. THE OTHER GUYS WILL NEVER BELIEVE ME WHEN I TELL THEM ABOUT THE ONE THAT GOT AWAY.

© 1987 United Feature Syndicate, I

EXPLOITATION FILMS PRESENTS

THE CAT THAT SAVED AMERICA

STARRING

MOTLEY

THE TIME: THE NOT-SO-DISTANT FUTURE. THE PLACE: A NATION ONCE PROUD AND FREE, NOW CALLED "AMERIKA" UNDER THE YOKE OF A COMMUNIST OPPRESSOR!

BUT THE RUSSKIES HADN'T COUNTED ON ONE THING — A PATRIOTIC GIANT CAT NAMED ....

MOTLEY!

HOORAY

HE'LL SAVE US FROM THE COMMIES!

WHERE ARE THOSE DIRTY REDS?

GO GET 'EM MOTLEY!

RATS! I'M TRAPPED IN THE TELEPHONE WIRES!

OH NO! IS THIS THE END OF MOTLEY?

4-5

GET OFF MY MODEL RAILROAD!!

UH OH! WE'LL NEVER BRING THIS IN UNDER BUDGET NOW!

© 1987 United Feature Syndicate, Inc.